COOL
MAKERSPACE
GADGETS & GIZMOS

ROBOTIFY IT!
ROBOTS YOU CAN MAKE YOURSELF

Elsie Olson

Checkerboard
Library

An Imprint of Abdo Publishing
abdopublishing.com

abdopublishing.com

Published by Abdo Publishing, a division of ABDO, PO Box 398166, Minneapolis, Minnesota 55439. Copyright © 2018 by Abdo Consulting Group, Inc. International copyrights reserved in all countries. No part of this book may be reproduced in any form without written permission from the publisher. Checkerboard Library™ is a trademark and logo of Abdo Publishing.

Printed in the United States of America, North Mankato, Minnesota
102017
012018

 THIS BOOK CONTAINS RECYCLED MATERIALS

Design: Sarah DeYoung, Mighty Media, Inc.
Production: Mighty Media, Inc.
Editor: Liz Salzmann
Cover Photographs: Mighty Media, Inc.; Shutterstock
Interior Photographs: iStockphoto; Mighty Media, Inc.; Shutterstock

The following manufacturers/names appearing in this book are trademarks: Energizer®, LEGO®, littleBits™, Sharpie®, 3M™

Publisher's Cataloging-in-Publication Data
Names: Olson, Elsie, author.
Title: Robotify it! robots you can make yourself / by Elsie Olson.
Other titles: Robots you can make yourself
Description: Minneapolis, Minnesota : Abdo Publishing, 2018. |
    Series: Cool makerspace gadgets & gizmos | Includes online
    resources and index.
Identifiers: LCCN 2017944035 | ISBN 9781532112553 (lib.bdg.) |
    ISBN 9781614799979 (ebook)
Subjects: LCSH: Robotics--Juvenile literature. | Creative ability in
    science--Juvenile literature. | Handicraft--Juvenile literature. |
    Makerspaces--Juvenile literature.
Classification: DDC 629.892--dc23
LC record available at https://lccn.loc.gov/2017944035

TO ADULT HELPERS

This is your chance to assist a young maker as they develop new skills, gain confidence, and make cool things! These activities are designed to help children create projects in makerspaces. Children may need more assistance for some activities than others. Be there to offer guidance when they need it. Encourage them to do as much as they can on their own. Be a cheerleader for their creativity.

Before getting started, remember to lay down ground rules for using tools and supplies and for cleaning up. There should always be adult supervision when using a hot or sharp tool.

SAFETY SYMBOLS

Some projects in this book require the use of hot or sharp tools. That means you'll need some adult help for these projects. Determine whether you'll need help on a project by looking for these safety symbols.

HOT!
This project requires the use of a hot tool.

SHARP!
This project requires the use of a sharp tool.

CONTENTS

What's a
MAKERSPACE?

Picture a place alive with excitement. All around you, creative crafters and techies in training are constructing amazing projects. Welcome to a makerspace!

Makerspaces are areas where people come together to create. They are the perfect places to make incredible **robotics** projects! Makerspaces are equipped with all kinds of materials and tools. But a maker's most important tool is his or her imagination. Makers find brand new ways to build their own robots. They find ways to put new twists on existing robotics projects. To do this, makers need to be creative problem solvers. Are you ready to become a maker?

BEFORE YOU GET STARTED

GET PERMISSION

Ask an adult for **permission** to use the makerspace and materials before starting any project.

BE RESPECTFUL

Share tools and supplies with other makers. When you're done with a tool, put it back so others can use it.

MAKE A PLAN

Read through the instructions and gather all your supplies ahead of time. Keep them organized as you create!

BE SAFE

Working with electricity can be **dangerous**, so be careful! Keep your power source switched off when connecting wires. Ask an adult for help when you need it.

WHAT IS A ROBOT?

A robot is a machine that is designed to do a job. Some robots operate **automatically**. Others are controlled remotely by people or computers. Robots come in all shapes and sizes. Some look like machines. Other robots are built to look like humans. Robots can do many jobs. They help build cars and vacuum floors. Some robots are toys that are fun to play with. There are several things to consider when creating robots and choosing materials to build them.

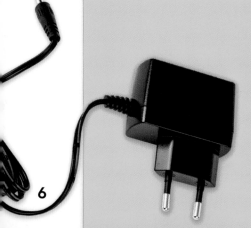

CIRCUIT POWER

A robot gets power from an electric circuit. A circuit is a closed loop that electricity can travel through. It needs a power source, such as a battery. It also needs a conductor, such as a wire. A circuit also has a load. This is a device the circuit powers, such as a light bulb. A switch opens and closes the circuit. This turns the power off and on.

LITTLEBITS

littleBits is a brand of electronic building blocks. littleBits parts include motors, power sources, and LED lights. The pieces are magnetic, so they're easy to fit together.

CUBELETS

Cubelets is another brand of electronic building blocks. They are cubes that connect to each other magnetically. Each type of block makes up part of the circuit. By connecting them in the right order, you can build many different types of circuits!

SUPPLIES

Here are some of the materials and tools used for the projects in this book. If your makerspace doesn't have what you need, don't worry! Find different supplies to substitute for the missing materials. Or modify the project to fit the supplies you have. Be creative!

chenille stems

craft foam

craft knife

Cubelets Six Kit

electrical tape

googly eyes

LEGO axle plate

LEGO basic bricks

LEGO plates

LEGO wheels

littleBits Gizmos & Gadgets Kit

littleBits UV LED bit

needle-nose pliers

9-volt battery

ROBOTIFY IT! TECHNIQUES

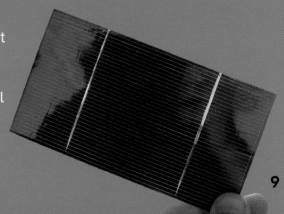

RED OR BLACK?

Batteries have negative and positive ends. Energy travels from the negative end toward the positive end. Because of this, many loads, such as motors, have negative and positive connectors. Positive connectors are usually red. Negative connectors are usually black. But not always! It's best to test your circuit before beginning a project so you know which parts are positive and which are negative.

SOLAR CELLS

Solar cells power devices by converting sunlight to electricity. Small, lightweight solar cells with wires already connected work best for most projects in this book. Before beginning a project, make sure the solar cell produces enough power for your motor. A 3-volt motor works best with at least a 3-volt solar cell. Also pay attention to the **milliamps** (mA) the cell generates. The higher the mA, the stronger the solar panel.

sandpaper

solar cell with wires

3V button battery

vibrating DC motor with wires

9

BOUNCY SOLAR BUGBOT

Build a jumping, jittery bug
powered by sunlight!

WHAT YOU NEED

2 round objects of different sizes, such as bowls or plastic lids • paper

pencil • scissors • craft foam • pushpin • ruler • solar cell with wires

double-stick adhesive foam • needle-nose pliers • 3 paper clips

hot glue gun & glue sticks • wire stripper • vibrating DC motor with wires

electrical tape • clear tape • googly eyes, chenille stems, pom-poms & other decorations

1. Find a round object that is larger than your solar cell. Set the object on a sheet of paper. Trace around it. This is the bug's body shape.

2. Set a smaller round object on the paper, **overlapping** the circle. Trace around the object. This is the bug's head shape. Cut along the outer lines of the shapes. This cutout is a **template**.

3. Place the template on a piece of craft foam. Trace around the template. Cut out the foam shape. This is the bug's body and head.

4. Use a pushpin to poke two holes in the bug's body. The holes should be about 1 inch (2.5 cm) apart.

5. Put several pieces of double-stick **adhesive foam** on the back of the solar cell. Do not put foam over the wires.

Continued on the next page.

6. Thread a solar cell wire through each of the holes in the bug's body. Press the solar cell to the center of the bug's body. Make sure the **adhesive foam** on the battery sticks to the foam bug body.

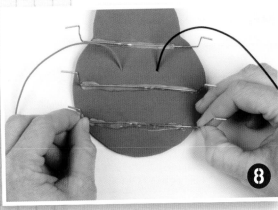

7 Use a needle-nose pliers to straighten three paper clips. These will be the bug's legs. Bend both ends of each paper clip to make feet.

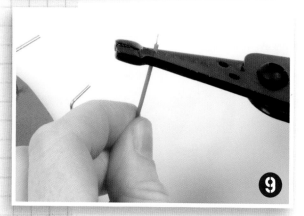

8 Turn the bug over so the solar panel faces down. Space the legs evenly across the body. Hot glue them in place.

9 Strip the ends of both solar cell wires and both motor wires.

10 Twist the positive solar cell wire and the positive motor wire together. Twist the negative solar cell wire and the negative motor wire together. Wrap electrical tape around each pair of twisted wires.

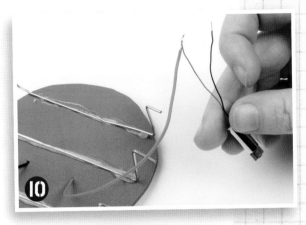

11 Use a small piece of double-stick **adhesive foam** to attach the motor to the bottom of the bug between the legs. Make sure the spinning part of the motor can move freely. Tape the solar cell and battery wires to the bug body so they don't stick out.

12. Decorate your bug! Add googly eyes and chenille stem antennae. Be creative!

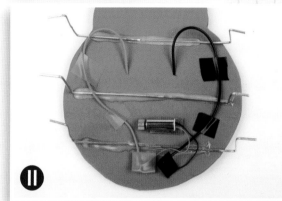

13. Set your bug outside in the sun. What happens when the sun hits the solar cell? The bug should vibrate and wiggle! If it doesn't, double check all wire connections.

TIP To strip a wire, place the wire stripper about ½ inch (1.25 cm) from the end of the wire. Gently squeeze the handles of the tool and pull the coating off the end of the wire.

BOT BRUSH HOVERBOARD

Make a mini hoverboard that will let a LEGO person scoot around!

1. Use the pliers to carefully break the head off the toothbrush.

2. Strip the ends of both motor wires. See page 13 for a tip on how to strip a wire.

3. Cut two pieces of double-stick **adhesive foam** about the size of the toothbrush head.

4. Stick one piece of adhesive foam to the back of the toothbrush head.

5. Stick the motor and positive wire to the adhesive foam. Make sure the spinning part of the motor hangs off one end of the toothbrush head and can move freely.

6. Stick the positive side of the battery on top of the positive wire. Make sure the stripped end of the wire touches the battery.

Continued on the next page.

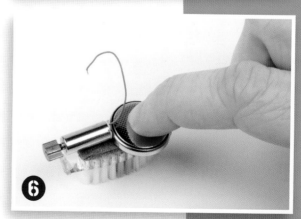

7. Test the motor. Touch the stripped end of the negative wire to the negative side of the battery. The motor should spin. If it doesn't, double check your connections or try turning the battery over.

8. Cut a 2-inch (5 cm) piece off the craft stick. Round off the piece's corners with a scissors. Sand the cut edges until they are smooth. This is the hoverboard.

9 Cover your work surface with newspaper. Paint one side of the hoverboard. Let the paint dry. Use paint pens to decorate the hoverboard. Let the paint dry.

10 Hot glue a 1×2 LEGO plate to the top of the hoverboard. Make sure the LEGO is in the center of the board. Let the glue dry.

11 Connect a LEGO person to the LEGO plate.

12 Stick the second piece of **adhesive foam** from step 3 to the bottom of the hoverboard. Make sure it is in the center of the board.

13 Stick the negative wire to the foam on the bottom of the hoverboard. Then stick the hoverboard to the top of the battery. When the stripped end of the wire is pressed by the hoverboard onto battery, the motor will spin!

14. If your hoverboarder tips over, try changing the placement of the hoverboard on the battery. Adjust the motor and battery placement, too, so the weight is balanced. Now sit back and watch your LEGO hoverboarder go!

TIP Instead of buying a motor, have an adult help you remove the vibrating motor from an old cell phone.

GUARD DROID

Build a daring droid to chase away intruders!

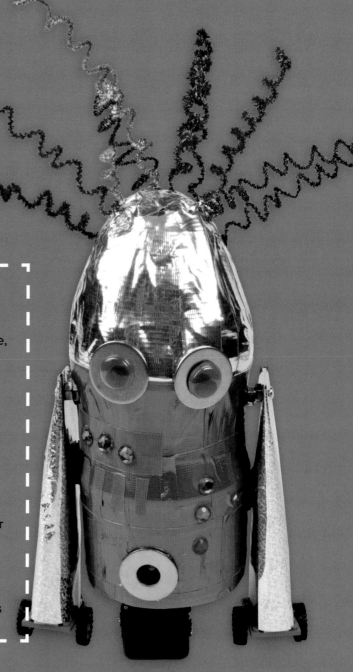

1. Connect the distance cube and the battery cube on either side of the drive cube. The **sensor** should face away from the drive cube.

2. Turn on the switch. Put your hand in front of the sensor. The cubes should move toward your hand. If they move away, turn the drive cube around.

3. Put the **passive** cube on top of the drive cube. Connect the flashlight cube to the top of the distance cube. The flashlight should face away from the passive cube.

4. Connect the 6×8 LEGO plate to the brick adapter. Connect the adapter to the top of the passive cube.

5. Cut the top third off the soda bottle. Set the open end over the top row of cubes. This is your **droid**'s body.

6. The LEGO plate should press against the sides of the bottle to hold it steady. Adjust the plate or add other LEGOs if necessary.

Continued on the next page.

7 Trace around the flashlight on the bottle. Have an adult help you carefully cut out the circle with a craft knife.

8 Carefully cut the foam ball in half with the craft knife. Duct tape one half to the bottom of the bottle.

9. Cover the bottom of the bottle in duct tape. Stuff tape into any empty spaces and cover them in more tape. Continue until the bottom of the bottle is a smooth **dome**.

10. Cover the rest of the **droid**'s body with duct tape. Don't cover the hole you cut in step 7.

11. Put two wheels on each **axle** plate. Connect each set of wheels to a 4×6 plate. Connect four 1×6 bricks in two rows to each 4×6 plate.

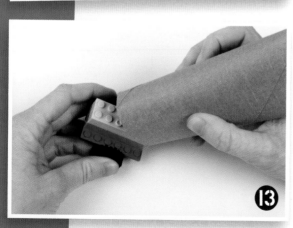

12. Cut two pieces of paper towel tube 6 inches (15 cm) long. Flatten one end of each tube and staple it.

13 Fit the open end of each tube over one of the wheel platforms. The tubes should fit tightly.

14. Cover the tubes with duct tape. Carefully use the craft knife to make a slit in the flat end of each arm. Push a paper fastener through each slit. These are the **droid**'s arms.

15. Put the droid body on the cubes and the entire structure on a flat surface. Hold one arm against the side of the droid. The wheels should rest on the flat surface. Mark where the fastener touches the droid. Repeat with the other arm.

16. Remove the droid body from the cubes. Use a craft knife to cut a slit at each mark. Put two nuts on the end of a fastener. Push the fastener ends through a slit in the droid's body. Bend the ends of the fastener ends against the inside of the body. Attach the other arm the same way.

17. Decorate your droid! Use hot glue to add googly eyes, gems, and more.

18. Set the droid back on the cubes. Turn on the switch. Watch your droid chase away unwelcome guests!

ROTATING ROBOT DESK PAL

Craft a spinning robot pencil holder!

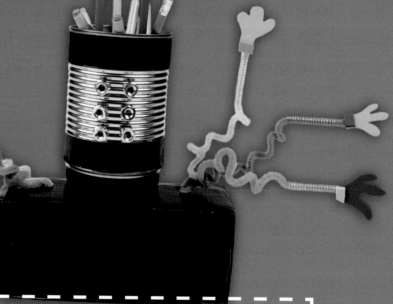

1. Connect the power bit to the slide dimmer bit. Connect the slide dimmer bit to the motor bit.

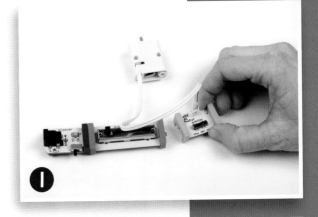

2. Snap the bits onto the mounting board near a long edge. Put the wheel on the motor's shaft. Connect the motor to the board across from the bits. The wheel should turn along the side of the board.

3. Connect the battery to the power bit. Attach the battery to the board with double-stick **adhesive foam**.

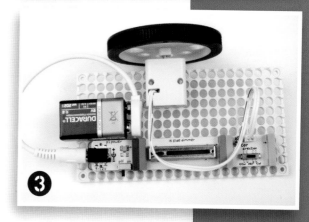

4. Turn on the power switch to test the circuit. Move the slide dimmer to make the wheel turn faster and slower. Turn off the switch.

5. Cut one large side off the box. Cut a *V* in the center of one long edge. Set the box on its side with the *V* on top.

6. Put the board in the box with the motor's shaft in the *V* and the wheel on the outside. The top of the board should touch the top of the box.

Continued on the next page.

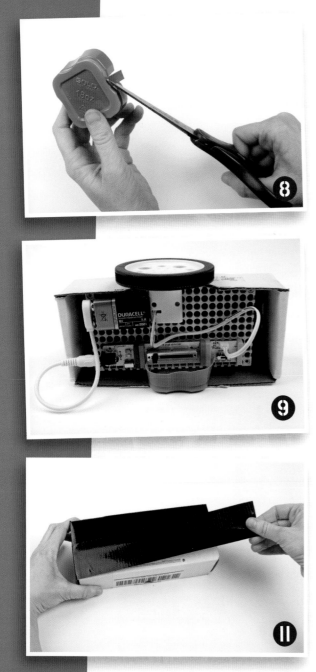

7. Measure the distance between the bottom of the board and the bottom of the box. Cut a piece 1 inch (2.5 cm) taller than the measurement off the bottom off a plastic cup.

8. Cut slots in two opposite sides of the cup. The slots should be 1 inch (2.5 cm) deep and wide enough for the mounting board to fit into. This is the stand for the board.

9. Remove the board from the box. Set it in the stand. Then slide the board back into the box.

10. Turn on the circuit and move the slide dimmer to make sure the wheel turns freely.

11. Remove the board from the box. Cover the outside of the box with duct tape. Don't put tape across the V.

12. Remove the label from the can. Decorate the can with strips of duct tape. Hot glue metal objects to it for decoration.

13 Bend each straw. Slide a spring onto the short end of each straw. Use googly eyes and craft foam to create two robot eyes. Hot glue one eye to the short end of each straw.

14 Tape the long end of each straw inside the can.

15. Cut six hands out of craft foam. Wrap each chenille stem around a pencil to make coils. Put a spring on one end of each coil. Hot glue a hand to the end of each spring.

16 Use a hole punch to make a hole in the box on each side of the *V*. Push the ends of three chenille stems through each hole. Bend the ends against the inside of the box. Tape them in place.

17. Put the mounting board back in the box. Put strips of double-stick **adhesive foam** on the bottom of the can. Press the can onto the wheel.

18. Fill your robot with pencils and pens. Turn on the power switch. Move the slide dimmer. Watch your robot spin!

MONSTER UNDER THE BED BOT

Make a motorized monster that only comes out when the lights are off!

WHAT YOU NEED

littleBits Gizmos & Gadgets Kit parts (power bit, light sensor bit, 2 DC motor bits, mounting board, 2 wheels, ball caster)

littleBits UV LED bit

9-volt battery

Glue Dot

double-stick adhesive foam

craft foam

ruler

scissors

scratch paper

marker

pushpin

googly eyes, pom-poms & other decorating materials

craft glue

craft knife

1. Connect the power bit to the light **sensor** bit. Connect the two motor bits to the light sensor bit. Connect the UV LED bit to the second motor bit.

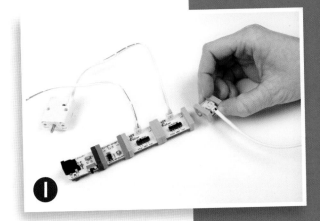

2. Snap the bits to the mounting board.

3. Put a wheel on each motor shaft. Snap the motors to the mounting board. Put one on each side of the light sensor bit. The wheels should turn freely along the sides of the board.

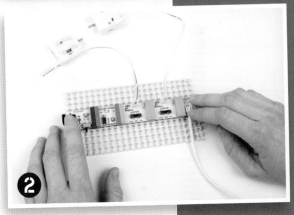

4. Set the light sensor bit to dark sensitivity mode. Set one wheel to "CCW" (counterclockwise). Set the other wheel to "CW" (clockwise).

5. Connect the battery to the power bit. Turn the power switch on to test the settings. When you shade the sensor, the light should turn on and the wheels should spin.

Continued on the next page.

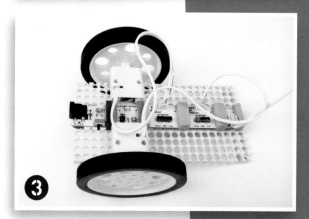

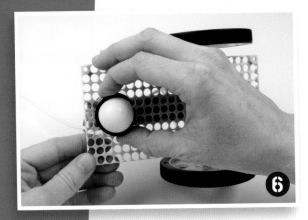

6. Use a Glue Dot to attach the ball caster to the bottom of the board. Center it under the UV LED light.

7. Attach the battery to the top of the mounting board with double-stick **adhesive foam**.

8. Cut a piece of craft foam that is 3¼ by 8½ inches (8 by 21.5 cm).

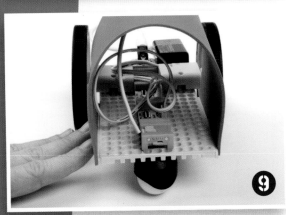

9. Cut two narrow strips of double stick adhesive foam 3¼ inches (8 cm) long. Stick them to the sides of the mounting board in front of the wheels. Press the ends of the craft foam rectangle to the adhesive foam. This is your monster's body.

10. Draw the shape of a monster face on scratch paper. It should be 3 inches (7.5 cm) wide and tall enough to cover the open end of the craft foam arc. Cut out the shape.

11. Trace the monster face shape on craft foam and cut it out.

12. Poke a hole near the top of the monster face with a pushpin.

13. Decorate your monster face with craft foam, googly eyes, and other materials.

14. Cut arms out of craft foam. Carefully use a craft knife to cut a slit on each side of the body. Stick an arm through each slit.

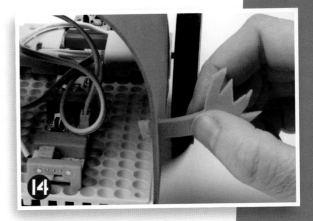

15. Cut a narrow piece of double-stick **adhesive foam** 3 inches (7.5 cm) wide. Stick it to the front edge of the mounting board. Cut several strips of double-stick foam. Stick them around the front edge of the craft foam body.

16. Push the LED light through the hole in the monster's face. Press the face to the adhesive foam strips on the front of the body and mounting board.

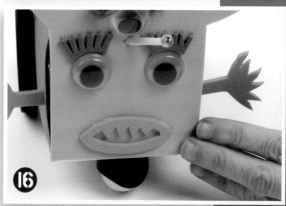

17. Decorate the monster's body! Use pom-poms and other materials.

18. Turn on your monster. Then turn off the lights. Watch your monster roll across the room! Try putting it under the bed and watch it scoot out.

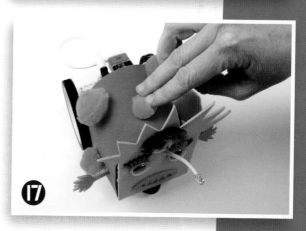

MAKERSPACE MAINTENANCE

Being a maker is not just about the finished craft. It's about communicating and **collaborating** with others as you create. The best makers also learn from their creations. They think of ways to improve them next time.

CLEANING UP

When you're done with a project, be sure to tidy up your area. Put away tools and supplies. Make sure they are organized so others can find them easily.

SAFE STORAGE

Sometimes you won't finish a project in one makerspace **session**. That's OK! Just find a safe place to store your project until you can work on it again.

MAKER FOR LIFE!

Maker project possibilities are endless. Get inspired by the materials in your makerspace. Invite new makers to your space. Check out what other makers are creating. Never stop making!

GLOSSARY

adhesive foam – craft foam that has one or more sticky sides.

automatic – moving or acting by itself.

axle – a bar that connects two wheels.

collaborate – to work with another person or group in order to do something or reach a goal.

dangerous – able or likely to cause harm or injury.

dome – a rounded top or roof that looks like half of a ball.

droid – short for "android," which is a robot that looks like a person.

milliamp – the electrical current produced at peak sunlight.

overlap – to lie partly on top of something.

passive – not active or without energy.

permission – when a person in charge says it's okay to do something.

robotics – the science of designing, constructing, and operating robots.

sensor – an instrument that can detect, measure, and transmit information to a controlling device.

session – a period of time used for a specific purpose or activity.

template – a shape or pattern that is drawn or cut around to make the same shape in another material.

INDEX